BIG BOOK OF CARS

Trevor Lord

DK PUBLISHING, INC.

A DK PUBLISHING BOOK

www.dk.com

Project Editor Carey Combe
Art Editors Mandy Earey
Claire Penny

US Editor Chuck Wills
Senior Editor Lin Esposito
Senior Art Editor Diane Thistlethwaite
Production Chris Avgherinos
Picture Research Liz Moore
Andrea Sadler
Photography Richard Leeney
Additional Photography Dave King

Jacket Design Piers Tilbury

First published in Great Britain in 1999
by Dorling Kindersley Limited, 9 Henrietta Street, London WC2E 8PS

First American Edition, 1999
2 4 6 8 10 9 7 5 3 1
Published in the United States by
DK Publishing, Inc.95 Madison Avenue, New York, New York 10016

Library of Congress Cataloging-in-Publication Data
DK big book of cars. -- 1st American ed.
p. cm.
Summary: Text and cut-out photographs present the features and performance of various cars, including the Corvette, Volkswagen Beetle, and Cadillac.
ISBN 0-7894-4738-X (alk. paper)
1. Automobiles Juvenile literature. [1. Automobiles.] I. DK Publishing, Inc.
TL206.B53 1999
629.222--dc21 99-25463
CIP

Colour reproduction by Colourscan, Singapore
Printed and bound in Spain by Artes Graficas, Mondadori
D.L. TO: 1198 - 1999

Dorling Kindersley would like to thank:
All Stretched Out; The Museum of British Road Transport, Coventry; Automobili Lamborghini; Chrysler Jeep Imports UK; Dennis Jacobs; Ford Motor Company; Garry Darby, American 50s Car Hire; Honda (UK); Kay Nelson; Mark Perkins at Karacter Kars; Mike Duke at South Bank University, London; Peugeot Motor Company PLC; Renault UK Ltd; Santa Pod Raceway; Society of Motor Manufacturers and Traders; Teresa Carnes; Toyota GB Ltd; Ty Bennett at NATMUS, Auburn, Indiana; Vauxhall; Volkswagen Group.

The publisher would like to thank the following for their kind permission to reproduce their photographs:

c=center, t=top, b=bottom, l=left, r=right

Allsport: 11tr; **Neill Bruce:** 3br, cr, 4t, 18tr, c, 25c, cr, 26tl, c, b, 27l, t, 30t, b, 31tl, tr, c; **Jeremy Davey:** 14c, b, 15c; **Ronald Grant Archive:** 18c, 19t, c, b; **Quadrant Picture Library:** 25t; **Rex Features:** 14tl

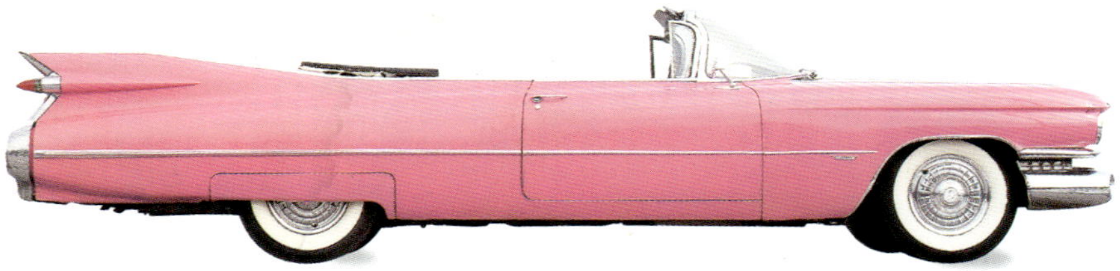

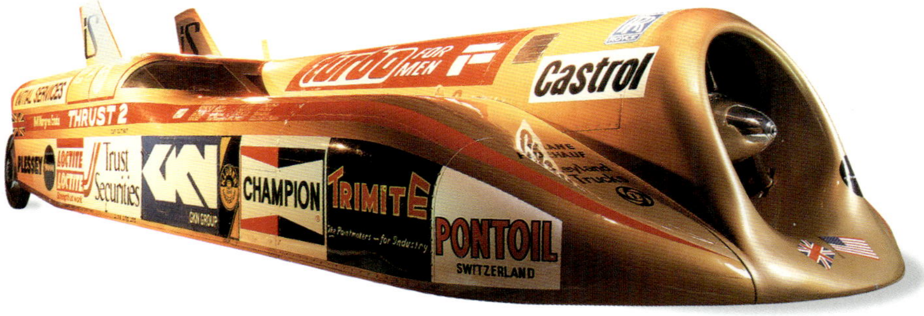
Castrol
CHAMPION
TRIMITE
PONTOIL
SWITZERLAND
THRUST 2

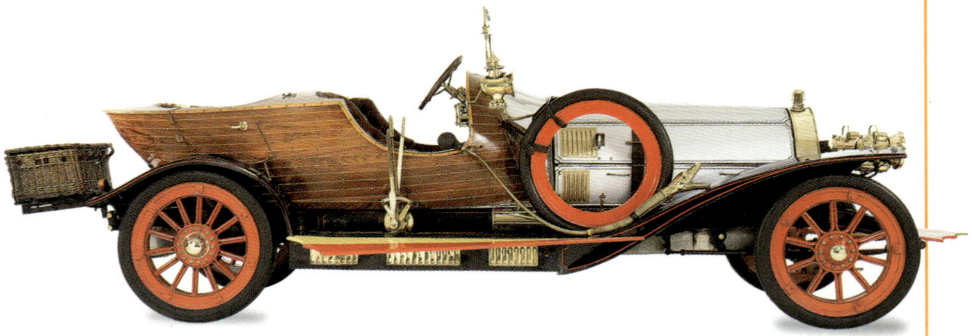

R-M
POWERGEN

Viper

Named after a dangerous type of snake, the Dodge Viper is one of the most spectacular cars ever built. It has an enormous engine which is more than six times bigger than the engine found in a small family car. In fact, it is one of the largest engines fitted to any car in the world, capable of taking the Viper to speeds exceeding 170 mph (274 kph). All big engines use a lot of fuel – driven fast the Viper only goes about six miles (two and half kilometers) on one gallon of gas!

Pickup engine
The engine for the Viper was converted from a pickup truck. The massive engine takes up a lot of room under the hood, so other equipment is squeezed into every available space.

On the track
The Viper is so fast that it is possible to use it for racing. It has successfully competed at races like the Le Mans 24 Hours in France, where it beat many "proper" racing cars.

The Viper hood ornament is a snake.

All engines need far more air than gas, and the Viper is no exception. With its huge engine, the Viper can use more than 5,000 gallons (20,000 liters) of air every minute. These vents direct the air through the radiator to cool the engine.

Tow car

Not many people would use a Viper to tow a trailer, but in 1998 someone gave it a try! The Viper managed to tow a trailer along an airport runway at more than 125 mph (204 kph) - setting a world record.

The car's curvy lines help its aerodynamics.

The Viper's huge 13-in-wide (33 cm) rear wheels allow the car to accelerate fast and corner quickly.

There are no door handles on a Viper. Instead, the doors are opened electronically by pressing buttons on the body.

These narrow headlights help give the car a viper-like appearance.

Powerful lights give greater visibility in thick fog.

The front spoiler stops air from going under the car and lifting it at high speed.

Lamborghini

The Italian tractor manufacturer Lamborghini started making cars less than forty years ago. Their cars have always been fast and spectacular. Lamborghinis are extremely complex – made out of incredibly expensive materials and parts. They are built so slowly and carefully that the factory only makes three cars a day, which explains why Lamborghinis are so rare and expensive.

Lamborghini Diablo
The Lamborghini Diablo is one of the world's most exotic, and expensive, sports cars. It is a supercar for the super-rich with a top speed of more than 206 mph (330 kph).

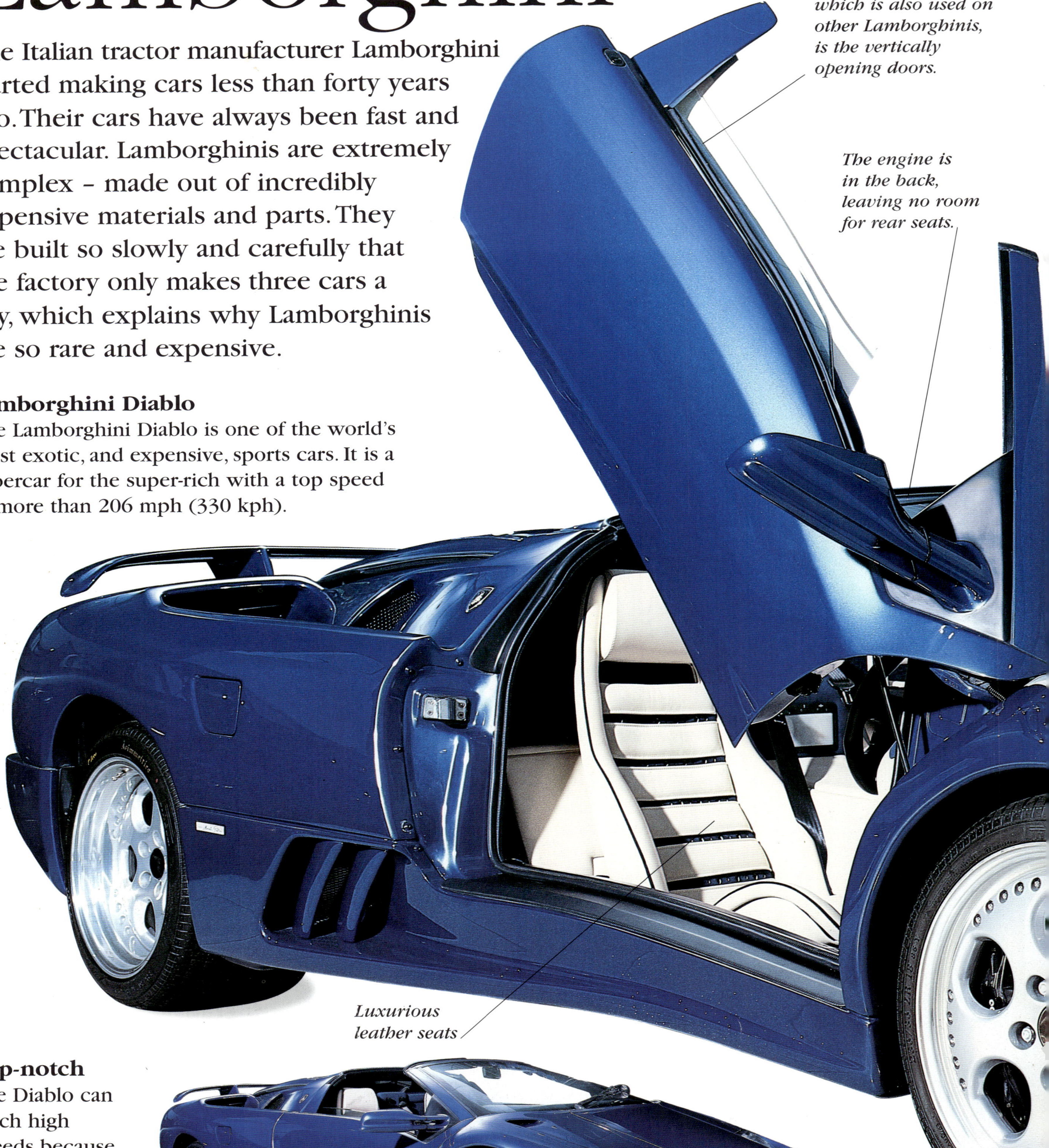

An unusual feature, which is also used on other Lamborghinis, is the vertically opening doors.

The engine is in the back, leaving no room for rear seats.

Luxurious leather seats

The large wheels are similar to those used on racing cars.

Top-notch
The Diablo can reach high speeds because of its advanced and powerful engine and its exceptionally aerodynamic body shape.

The large rear wing helps keep the car stable at 206 mph (330 kph).

The powerful 1.5-gallon (5.7-liter) engine can accelerate the Diablo from standstill to 60 mph (100 kph) in under four seconds.

Careful reversing!
The reverse gear on the Diablo is for parking and turning the car around, just like on other cars. But drivers should take special care when backing the Diablo into a small parking space – the car will do more than 60 mph (100 kph) in reverse!

The Diablo is available with an open top or a fixed roof.

The Lamborghini emblem – a bull on a black background – can also be found on the company's tractors.

The ground clearance at the front can be adjusted by the driver.

Volkswagen Beetle

The idea for the first Beetle came from Adolf Hitler. He wanted a car that was very cheap to buy and easy to maintain – a people's car or, in German, a Volkswagen. He asked engineer Ferdinand Porsche to design it for him, and the car was put into production in the 1940s. It proved so popular that it became the best-selling car ever.

Beetle concept
The new Beetle has been built by combining today's technology with the looks and style of Porsche's design. If you see one, you will notice that the car has an amazing ability to make just about every other car on the road look old fashioned, even though it is based on a design that is more than 60 years old!

New Beetle
Volkswagen calls this new Beetle the New Beetle! This new car is similar to the original Beetle, but it is nearly five times as powerful as the first Beetle and will go twice as fast. There is another big difference – the first Beetle had the engine at the back.

Volkswagen's famous emblem

The plastic bumpers spring back into shape after small impacts.

Beetle convertible
Volkswagen made 60 original Beetle sedans for every convertible, so the open-top version is quite rare today. The convertible's body was made by taking a brand-new sedan, stripping it, and then cutting off the roof!

Beetle interior
The large speedometer behind the steering wheel is similar to the type found in the old Beetles, but on this one the needle is red and the background glows blue. Less space-age is the flower vase, which is fitted as standard to every car.

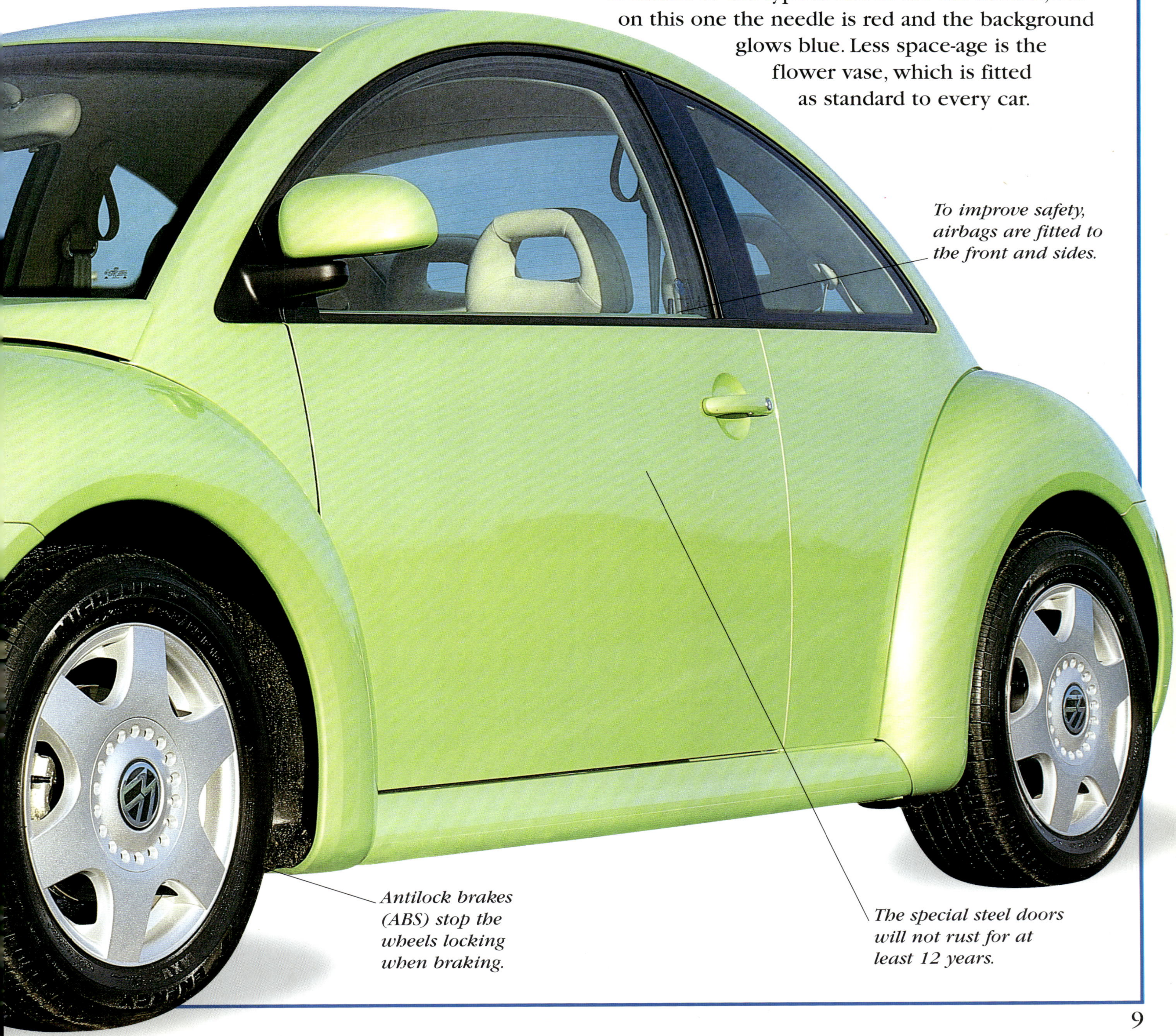

To improve safety, airbags are fitted to the front and sides.

Antilock brakes (ABS) stop the wheels locking when braking.

The special steel doors will not rust for at least 12 years.

Dragsters

Drag racing started in the USA. The original competitions took place on public roads using traffic lights to start the race. The cars would race along a straight road to an agreed marker to see which car could accelerate the fastest. These races were not only very dangerous, but also illegal – so special *drag strips* were built, and the sport of drag racing was born.

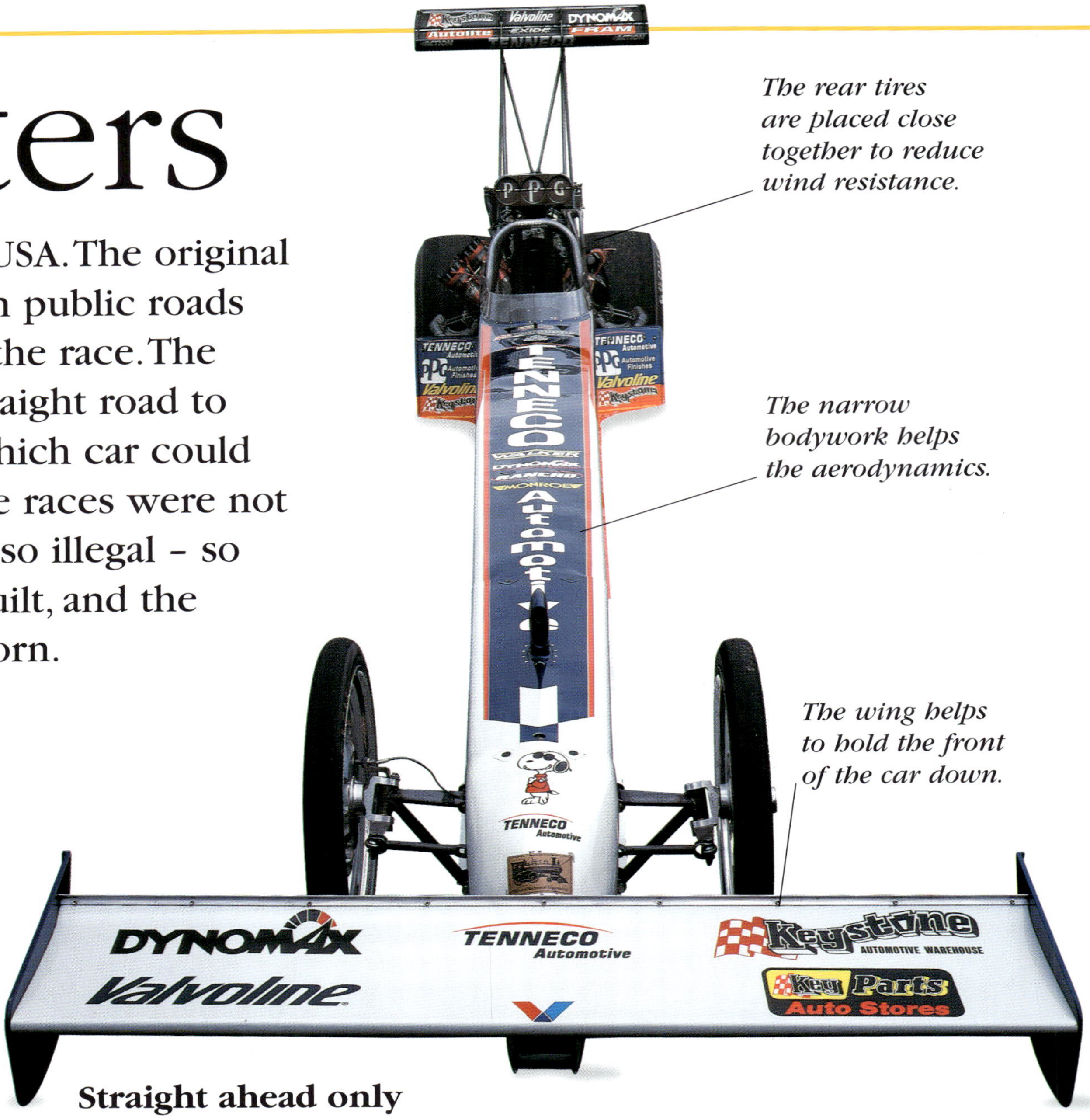

The rear tires are placed close together to reduce wind resistance.

The narrow bodywork helps the aerodynamics.

The wing helps to hold the front of the car down.

When the dragster is moving, air pressure on the rear wing pushes the car down to get more grip from the tires.

Straight ahead only

Racing cars are very wide because it helps them to go around corners, but dragsters always race in a straight line so the cars can be narrow to reduce wind resistance. They are also very long, which helps to stop the front from lifting when they start accelerating.

The driver and engine are both at the back of the car to help put weight on the tires for extra grip.

A rollbar helps protect the driver if the car turns over.

The "wheelie bar" stops the front of the dragster being lifted too much by the airflow under the car.

Expensive materials

Dragsters – like race cars, speedboats, and airplanes – need to be very light and strong. A good design is important, but so is using new, modern materials like titanium, magnesium, kevlar, and carbon fiber to help save weight. Unfortunately, they are all very expensive.

Sponsorship helps pay the huge costs involved in drag racing.

Safety first

A dragster driver wears the most up-to-date safety clothing, including a flameproof suit in case the dragster bursts into flames after a crash.

Smoking tires!

To accelerate quickly it is important that the huge rear tires give as much grip as possible. The tires grip best when they are very hot, so the drivers spin them on water before the race to heat them up – the water helps to start the tires spinning.

The airbox sits right up at the top to collect air for the engine.

There are no mufflers on the exhausts, so dragsters are very loud.

Dragster engines

Top dragsters use the most powerful engines in all motorsports – eight times as powerful as the engines used in Formula One cars. All races are a quarter of a mile (400 meters) long. The dragster's huge power allows it to cover the required distance, from standstill, in less than 5 seconds. But the wear on the cars means they need to be rebuilt after just one race!

The rear tires are inflated to just 20 percent of normal pressure to help with grip.

A parachute is stored here to stop the car at the end of a race.

The wide rear tires last just 4 runs – that's just 20 seconds of use!

A top dragster uses 15 gallons (60 liters) of fuel racing just a quarter of a mile (400 metres)!

The front wheels have little to do, so they can be very small to save weight.

Pink Cadillac

At a time when American cars were big and luxurious, the Cadillac was the biggest and most luxurious of all. This convertible version cost three times as much as a family car. It was made when air travel by jet was just starting and was designed to attract attention by looking like a jet plane. It attracted even more attention when it was pink!

Cadillac interior
Everything was done to make driving the Cadillac as effortless as possible. Adjusting the seat, lowering the roof, and opening the trunk were all done electrically. Even the headlights dimmed automatically!

There is room inside for six people to sit in comfort.

A Cadillac was the first car to be fitted with twin headlights.

The surrounds of the lights resemble the air intake of a jet engine.

This car is almost 20 feet (6 meters) long and 6 feet (1.8 meters) wide – huge when compared with today's cars.

Cadillac

Cadillacs were popular with singers and movie-stars. In the 1980s an American rock star recorded a song called *Pink Cadillac*.

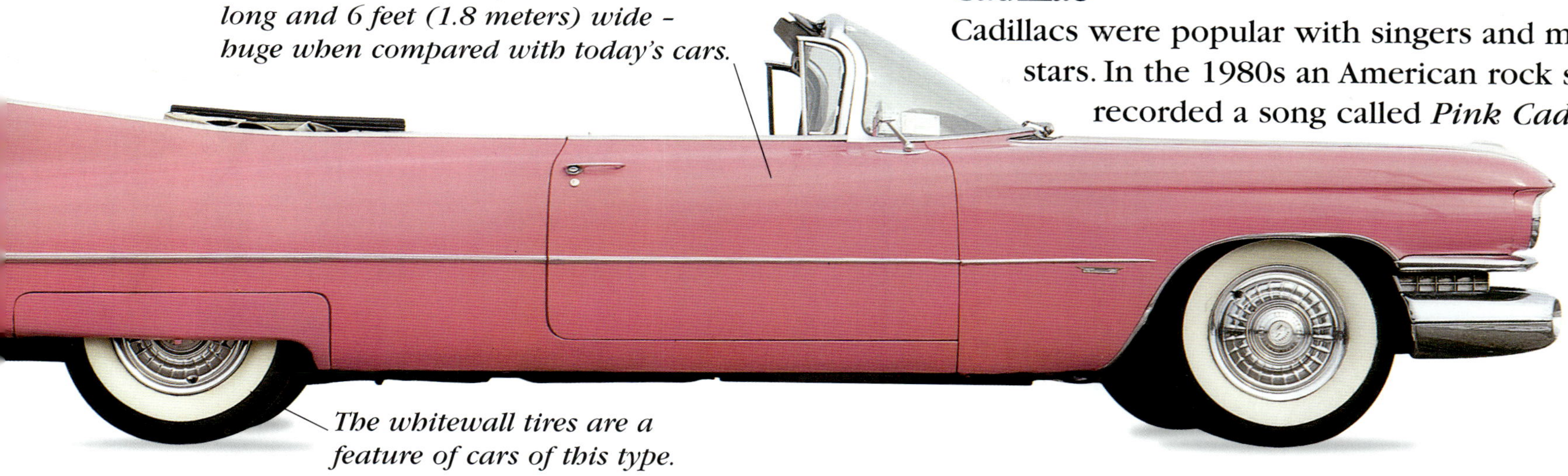

The whitewall tires are a feature of cars of this type.

Cadillac fins

Fins were very popular on 1959 American cars, and this Cadillac Convertible has the biggest fins of them all. At their highest point they are 42 inches (106 centimeters) from the ground and – like the fins on all cars – they serve no purpose other than for styling.

The rear lights are designed to look like bullets.

Cadillac designs changed every year. This one is from 1959.

There are two grilles, one on top of the other in "double-decker" style.

Thrust

Two Thrust cars have held the Land Speed Record. But when ThrustSSC (SuperSonic Car) became the fastest car ever on October 15th, 1997, at a speed of more than 763 mph (1,228 kph), it also broke the sound barrier – the first car ever to do so.

Breaking the sound barrier
Try to imagine this: ThrustSSC is driving toward you, but you can't hear it until after it has gone past. This is because the car is traveling faster than the sound it is making – i.e., faster than the speed of sound! But attempting to break the sound barrier in a car was potentially very dangerous – no one knew how a car would behave at such high speeds.

The driver sits between the engines.

ThrustSSC
ThrustSSC is powered by two Rolls-Royce Spey jet engines, which together are three times as powerful as the single engine used in Thrust 2.

The rear wing helps to keep the car stable at the speed of sound.

Hot air leaving the jet engine at very high speed pushes the car along.

The two large engines don't leave enough room to allow the front wheels to steer the car, so ThrustSSC is steered by a single rear wheel.

Thrust 2

The British driver of Thrust 2, Richard Noble, took the land speed record from American Gary Gabelich. Thrust 2 held the Land Speed Record for 14 years at 633 mph (1,018 kph). Noble then went on to build ThrustSSC.

The driver sits to one side of the central jet engine.

Sponsors' advertising helps pay for expensive record-breaking!

The wheels are made of solid aluminum so they do not explode or disintegrate at very high speed.

Thrust team

A project to set the Land Speed Record and to be the first to break the sound barrier takes years of planning and preparation. It also takes an enormous amount of money and a large team of dedicated, talented, and hard-working people. From driver Andy Green, a pilot with Britain's Royal Air Force, to the designers, engineers, cooks, and accountants – every member of the team had a very important job.

Air is sucked into the jet engine this end.

The very sharp nose cuts through the air easily.

Corvette

The American car company Chevrolet has been making Corvettes since 1953. The Corvette is the world's best-selling sports car, and the latest model – which can reach 173 mph (280 kph) – is the most exciting of them all. This Corvette can accelerate from a standstill to 60 mph (100 kph) in less than five seconds.

Side protection
Both doors are filled with a new type of impact-resisting foam and fitted with steel beams. These safety measures give the driver and passenger extra protection in a crash.

No spare wheel

To reduce weight and give more luggage space, there is no jack or spare wheel. If one of the special tires is punctured, the Corvette can still be driven for up to 100 miles (160 kilometers), even if the tire has lost all its air.

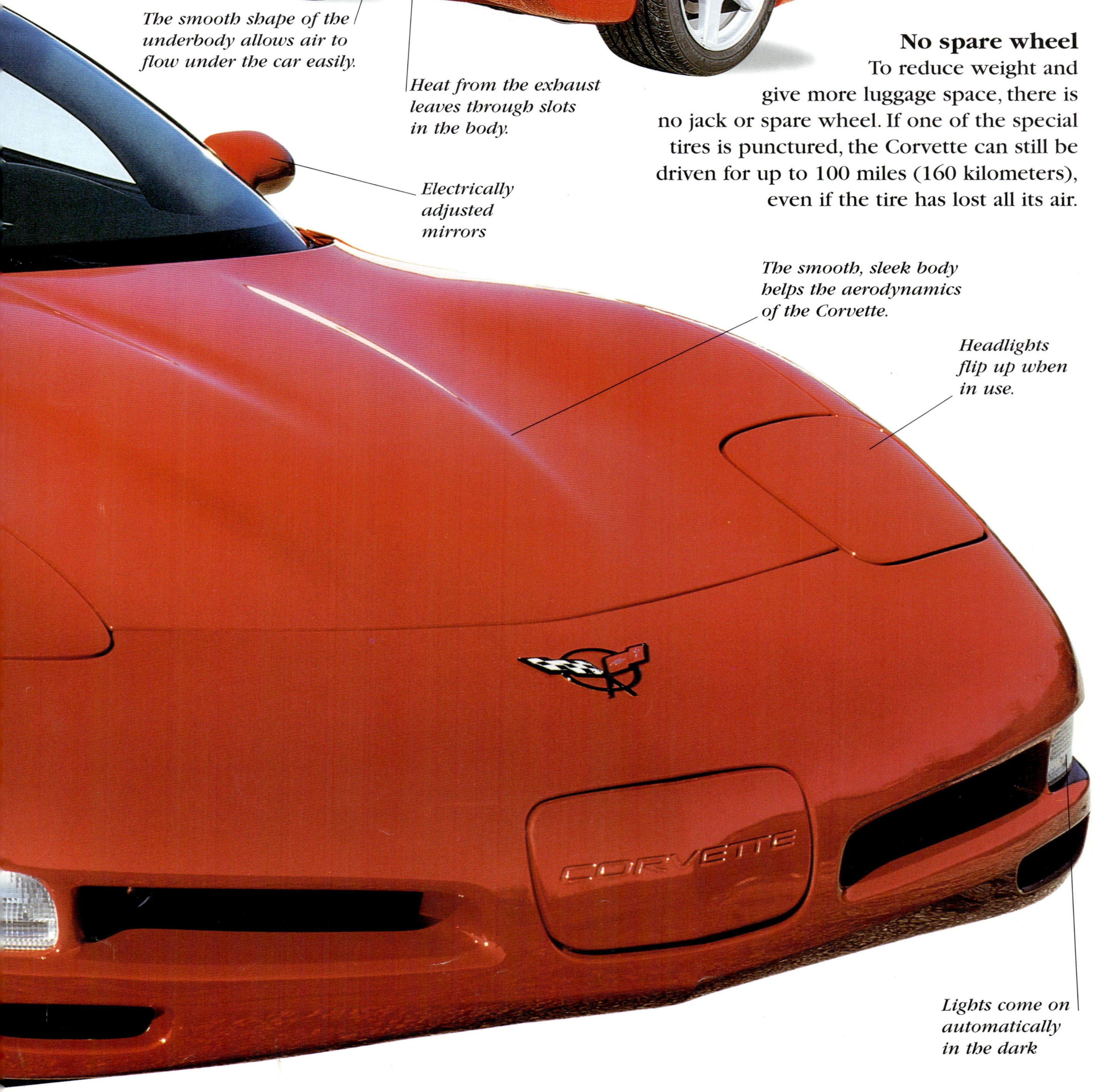

Stretch four-wheel-drive limousine
This car was based on a big, American, off-road, four-wheel-drive car. The extra wheels at the back give the car even more grip – although it is no longer used for off-road driving!

Limousine interior
The interior has a large and lavish drink and snack area.

This car has more ground clearance than most limousines.

This rear door was part of the original car.

This long section with windows was added to the original car.

Stretch limousine

The word "limousine" is often used to describe any large, chauffeur-driven car, but these "stretched" limousines must be the ultimate in road-going luxury. They are built by taking a standard car, cutting it in half, and adding a long center section.

Longest limousine in Europe
Europe's longest rental limousine comes from one of its smallest countries – Wales. It is based on an American Lincoln. After the conversion, the car was almost 40 feet (12 meters) long!

It is difficult to make a very long body strong enough to stop it from bending in the middle!

Shining example
Stretch limousines are too long to go through a car wash, so they have to be cleaned by hand. To make this car spotlessly clean inside and out takes one person two days!

A television antenna for the three TV sets inside.

Jazzy lights add to the glitzy feel!

Heart-shaped windows

Extra set of wheels to support the back of the car.

Star cars

The first movie theater and the first car appeared in England at about the same time – just over one hundred years ago. From the very beginning of the movies, cars have featured in films. In recent years, some of these amazing cars have found greater stardom than the actors!

Bond, James Bond

James Bond's cars are always equipped with lots of incredible gadgets and can do some amazing things. The most famous is the DB5 Aston Martin, used in the movie *Goldfinger*.

Fear of flying

Passengers in Bond's Aston Martin should avoid upsetting him. With just the flip of a switch, the passenger seat (and passenger) can be sent hurtling through the roof and high into the air!

The taillight can spread oil on to the road.

The bulletproof shield can be raised to protect Bond from gunfire.

Bond can use the bumper overriders as battering rams.

The exhaust pipe can produce a smoke screen.

Guns come out of the headlights.

Chitty Chitty Bang Bang

The star of the movie *Chitty Chitty Bang Bang* was based on a real car that raced in Britain during the 1920s. It got its name from the noisy engine that went chitty-chitty-bang-bang!

Wings and all

This original poster shows why Chitty Chitty Bang Bang is such a magical car – it can fly!

The two huge headlights can light the night sky.

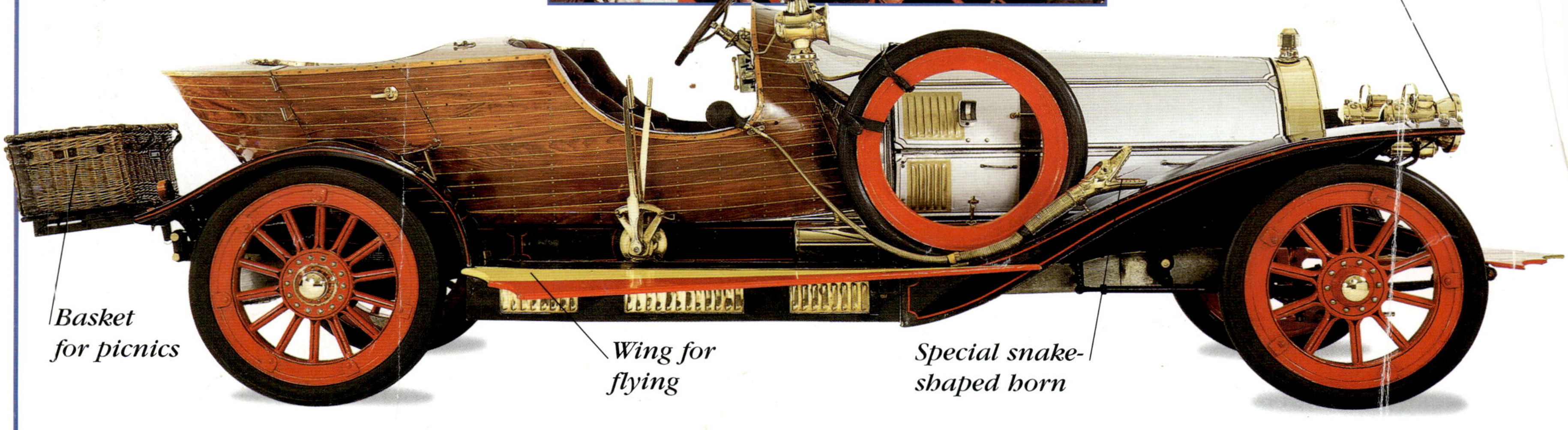

Basket for picnics

Wing for flying

Special snake-shaped horn

The Batmobile

The *Batmobile* first appeared in a comic strip, it wasn't until a few years later that it was brought to life in the 1960s television series. The futuristic design – such as the aircraft-style windshield – was based on a Ford concept car called the Lincoln Futura.

rtist's impression

nis is an artist's impression a very unusual Batmobile. lthough it has four wheels ke an ordinary car, its unique eature is that they are arranged n a single line like a bicycle.

atman Returns

n the movie *Batman Returns*, the Batmobile as to shrink so that it can drive down a narrow lley. To do this, they removed the side wings nd pulled in the wheels o it looked just like the ketch above. They then witched the cars uring filming.

Convertible Mercedes-Benz

It is very hard to build a stretch limousine without a roof, as a roof makes a car much stronger. The designer of this car, however, not only managed to make the car strong enough not to need a roof, but he also made it capable of taking the weight of a swimming pool at the back!

The eight rear wheels are needed to support the weight of the swimming pool.

There is room inside for ten people to sit back and relax.

The pink color helps the car to stand out from the crowd!

With such a long car, it is important that the driver is very good at parking!

Disco on wheels

The interior of this Lincoln limousine has all the features you would expect to find in a nightclub. The interior lights flash in time to the music from the CD player, there are three video screens, and even a game machine. Dancing, however, may be a problem!

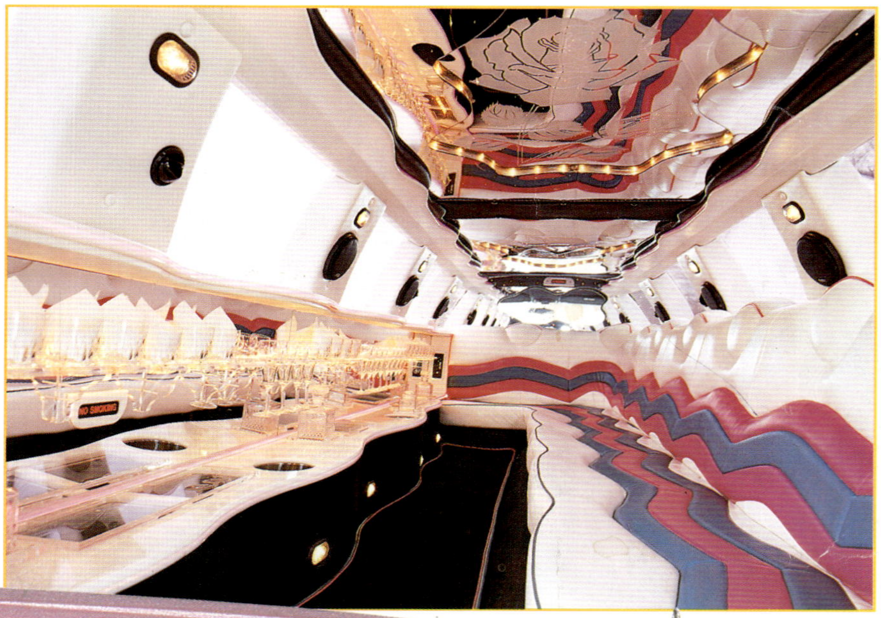

There is a sliding door behind the driver's seat, so passengers can talk to the driver.

The tires need higher pressure than normal to cope with the extra weight.

A close study of the back of this car shows that the long compartment has been made by taking the tail sections from two cars, including their wheels, and joining them together.

Hotel on wheels

Limousines are not usually used for long journeys, but if the passengers in this one were tired, all they would need to do is curl up on the huge double bed at the back of the car!

Space to spare

There is room for more than 15 people to sit comfortably inside this limousine, together with their luggage and even a dog or two!

The windows of limousines are often black to protect the privacy of the people inside.

This car is four times as long as a small sedan.

Solar cars

Solar cars use sunlight for fuel. Panels collect the sunlight and convert it into electricity. This is used to power the electric motors. Electricity stored in batteries can be used for short distances when there are low levels of sunlight. Solar cars may be expensive to build, but they are quiet, they cause no pollution – and sunlight is free!

World Solar Challenge
Blessed with lots of sunshine, Australia is the ideal place to race solar cars. Every three years the World Solar Challenge takes place with the cars driving 1875 miles (3,000 km) from Darwin to Adelaide at speeds of up to 53 mph (85 kph).

Mad Dog
Mad Dog, designed by staff and students at a London university, is Britain's most successful solar-powered car. It was named after the famous song by Noel Coward – "Mad Dogs and Englishmen."

Mad Dog can cruise at more than 44 mph (70 kph) – as long as it stays sunny!

Mad Dog only has space for one person.

The aerodynamic windshield reduces wind resistance to save energy.

Mad Dog is very light so that it uses less energy. The frame is made from carbon fiber, so the car – even with the heavy batteries – weighs only as much as a motorcycle.

Without sponsorship, Mad Dog would never have been developed.

Motorcycle wheels are used because they are both light and strong.

Honda Dream

Honda builds experimental cars to gain the information needed to develop the cars we will be driving in the future. The *Dream* is the fastest solar-powered car in the world, and is capable of reaching speeds of more than 88 mph (140 kph).

There is room for two people to sit, one behind the other.

The left rear wheel is the only one driven by the motor.

Toyota Skyliner

Toyota's *Skyliner* is a concept vehicle that uses a clever combination of solar energy and electricity. Wheels mounted on the wings allow the car to be driven on roads using solar energy. But in congested cities, the wings can be folded upward to attach the car to an overhead electric rail.

Solar panels collect the sun's energy.

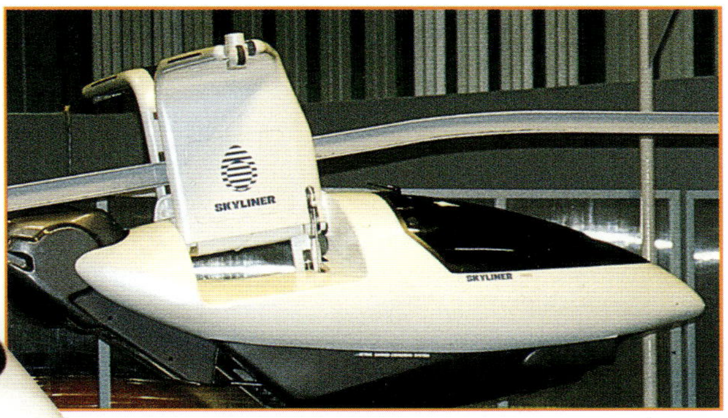

High in the sky

Attached to rails high in the sky, the *Skyliner* could travel above the crowded roads.

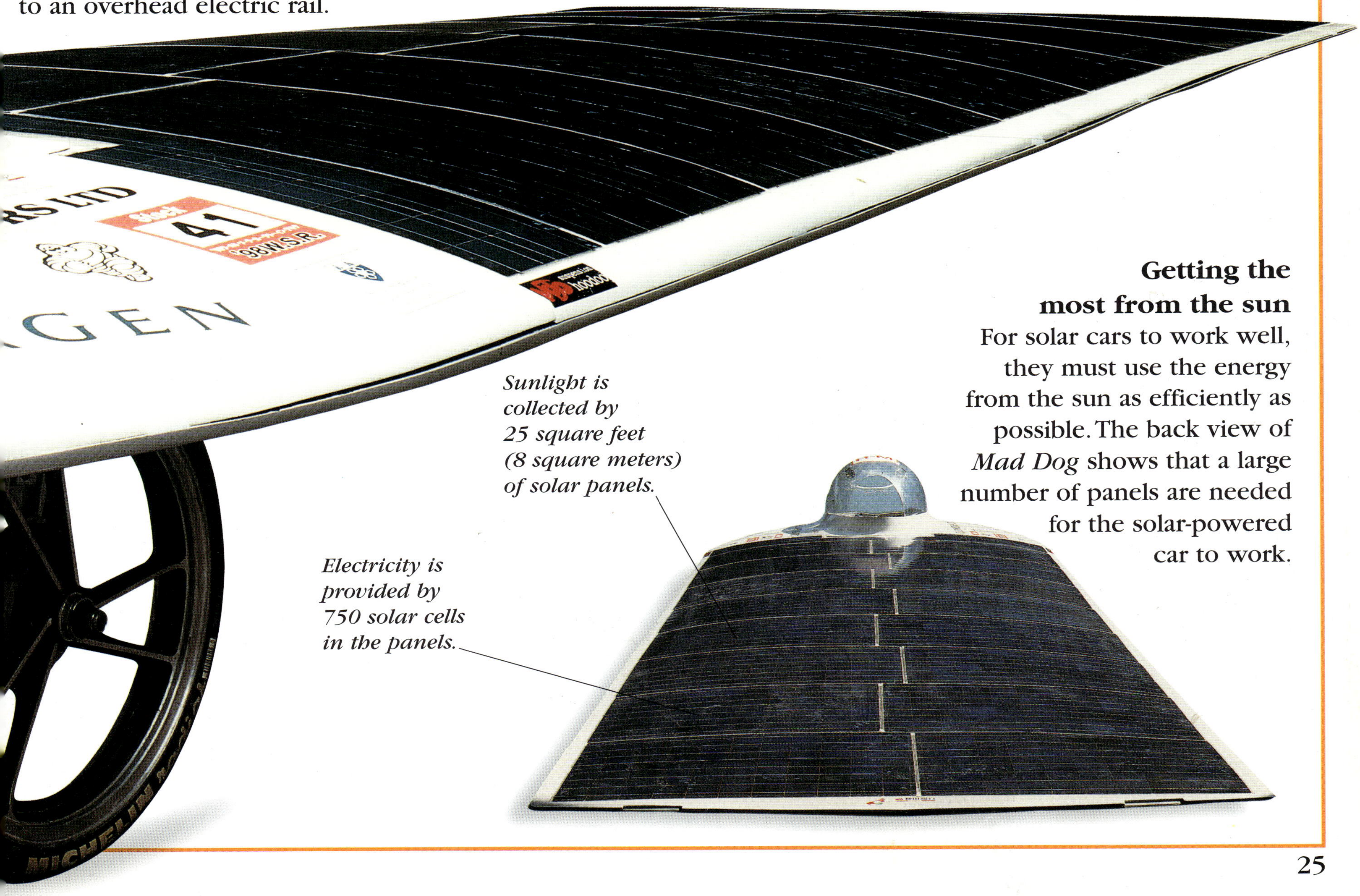

Getting the most from the sun

For solar cars to work well, they must use the energy from the sun as efficiently as possible. The back view of *Mad Dog* shows that a large number of panels are needed for the solar-powered car to work.

Sunlight is collected by 25 square feet (8 square meters) of solar panels.

Electricity is provided by 750 solar cells in the panels.

Ford concept cars

As one of the largest car manufacturers in the world, Ford is always looking to the future. To show new ideas to the public, Ford builds concept cars. These cars are not built to be sold, they are built to show the public what cars might look like in the future, and what they might be capable of doing. Some are made to work; others are just for show.

1996 Ford Ghia Saetta
The Saetta is based on the Ford Ka, a small hatchback. It shows how components from one model can be used to make a completely different type of car.

Ford Synergy 2010
If cars can be made to use less fuel, they will be cheaper to run and will cause less pollution. The idea of the Synergy is to show how, by the year 2010, cars could use just one-third of the fuel consumed today.

There is room inside for a family of six.

The Synergy has a unique double door.

The all-glass roof is coated so that it reflects heat in the summer and saves heat in the winter. This reduces the need for heating and air-conditioning.

The streamlined shape is 40% more aerodynamic than today's cars.

The rear wheel cover, or "spat," makes the car more aerodynamic.

Synergy 2010 interior

There are no switches on the dashboard. The driver operates all the electronic controls by talking to the car! There are no dials, either. Instead, the information is projected onto glass in front of the driver.

The 1995 Ford Indigo

The Ford Indigo concept car brings Formula One style and technology to the road. The front wing is designed so that the air flowing over it pushes the car down – giving the wide tires extra grip. The engine is positioned behind the driver, just as it is in a racing car. Many of the parts are made of carbon fiber, which is light, strong, and very expensive.

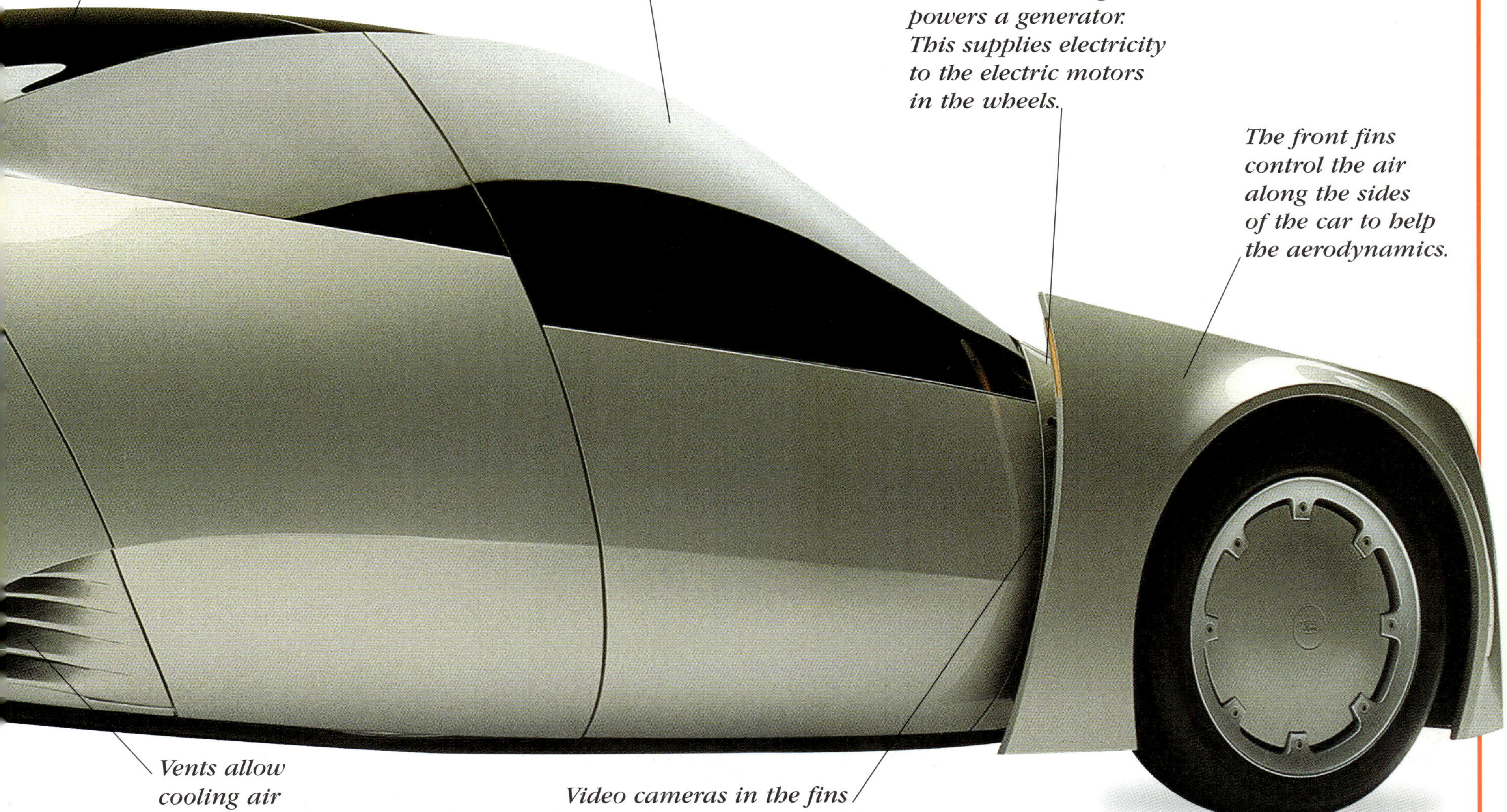

The Slug

Is this what cars will look like in the future? The designers of the Slug think that by the year 3000 all cars will be driven by computers. Computer-controlled cars could travel in tightly packed convoys. Without drivers to make mistakes, they could reach speeds of more than 200 mph (480 kph) in complete safety. This system would also save road space, which means that fewer new roads would need to be built.

Slug drive

The Slug gets its name from the way it moves. Instead of wheels, it has an underbody - known as the slug-drive - that can change shape to propel the vehicle forward - just like a slug.

The solar panel provides electricity. It can move to follow the Sun when the car is parked.

Smooth shape

With a computer to do the driving, the slug has no need for lights, indicators, or mirrors on the outside of its body. It doesn't need a windshield or windows either, because not only can the Slug drive itself, it can also navigate – leaving the occupants free to do other things.

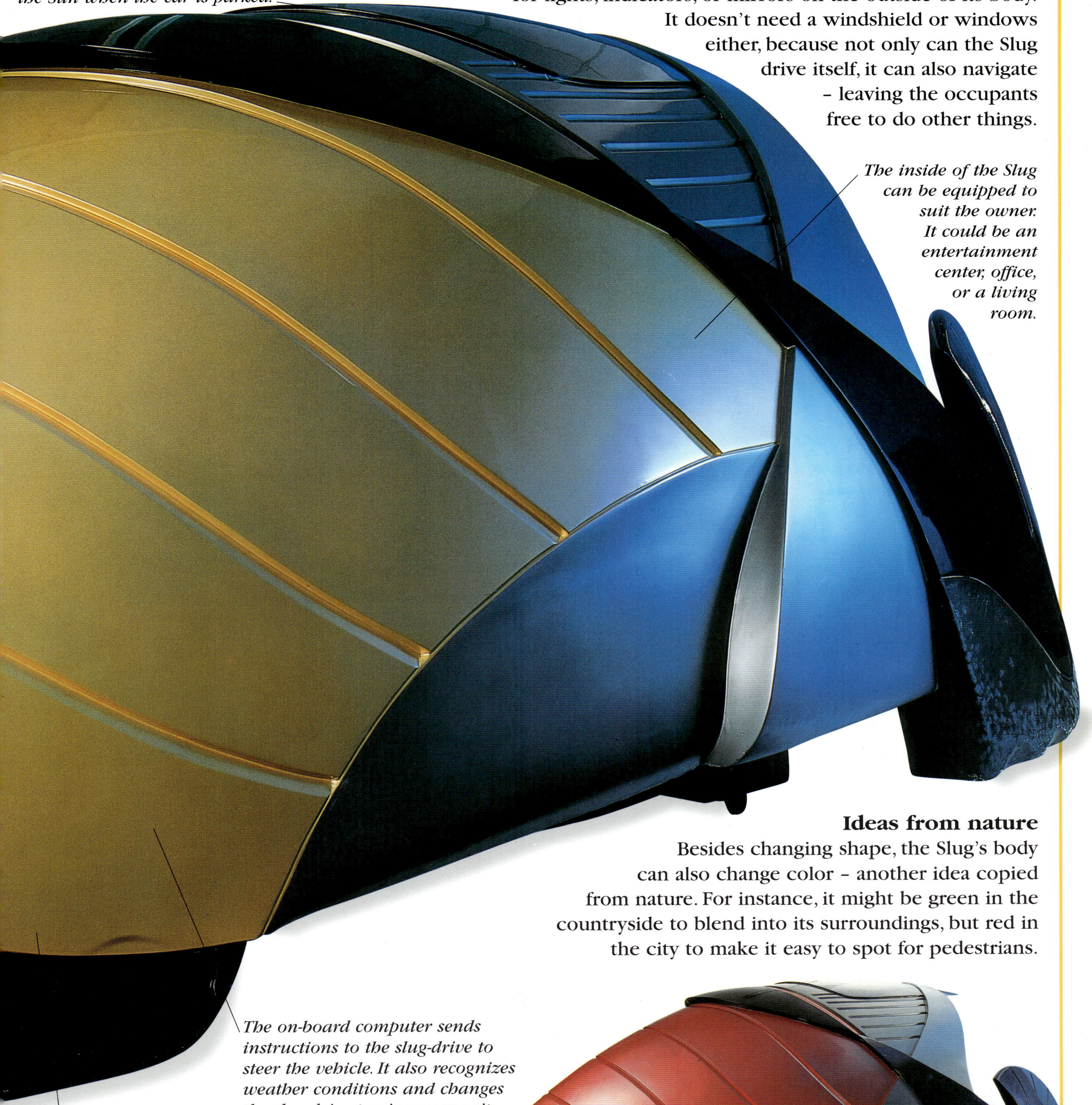

The inside of the Slug can be equipped to suit the owner. It could be an entertainment center, office, or a living room.

Ideas from nature

Besides changing shape, the Slug's body can also change color – another idea copied from nature. For instance, it might be green in the countryside to blend into its surroundings, but red in the city to make it easy to spot for pedestrians.

The on-board computer sends instructions to the slug-drive to steer the vehicle. It also recognizes weather conditions and changes the slug-drive to give more grip when the road is slippery.

The front slides back to allow passengers to get in or out.

Into the future

With our roads becoming more and more crowded and the pollution from cars continuing to damage the environment, driving in the future will have to be very different from how we do it today. Nobody knows what cars will look like a hundred years from now, but designers and engineers are working hard to find ways to solve the problems.

Toyota Shaker
Instead of wheels, the *Shaker* has hundreds of plastic rods attached to the underside of the body. The rodsare positioned so that when they vibrate they push the vehicle forward. A system like this would not give a very comfortable ride and would certainly live up to its name – perhaps it's back to the drawing board on this one!

Peugeot Touareg
Peugeot thinks that the cars of the future should be fun. The *Touareg* is a four-wheel-drive vehicle that allows the driver to enjoy off-road thrills. It has an electric motor so there are no exhaust fumes and no noise – apart from the people inside enjoying themselves!

The large clearance between the wheels and the bodywork prevents clogging by mud or sand.

There are no doors or roof – you just jump in. Let's hope it doesn't rain!

The wheels and tires are made to look as though they are one solid piece.

Renault Zoom

One of Renault's ideas for a city car of the future is the *Zoom*. This electrically powered car is ideal for town use because the rear wheels can move forward to make the car shorter – making it easier to park.

The smooth shape protects pedestrians during a crash.

The rear wheels are extended for driving.

Special paint work means that any scratches on the bodywork can be removed by just polishing.

The driver hears a warning inside the car if the tires start to go flat

The rear wheels are in position for parking

The Touareg gets its name from a nomadic people who live in the desert.

The body is molded from carbon fiber.

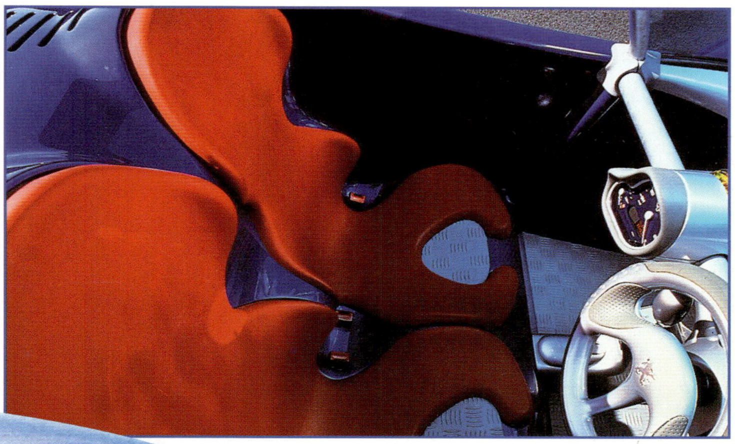

Easy-to-clean interior

The seats and interior of the *Touareg* are all made of plastic, so they can be cleaned using a garden hose!

Glossary

Aerodynamic
A shape that can move through the air easily.

Air bag
A device that quickly inflates to prevent car passengers from hitting the windshield during an accident.

Aluminum
A very light and strong metal.

Antilock brakes (ABS)
A braking system that stops the wheels from skidding.

Carbon fiber
Similar to glass fiber but lighter, stronger, and more expensive.

Concept car
A car built to demonstrate new and often unusual ideas.

Convertible
A car with a fabric roof that can be lowered.

Dashboard
The panel at the front of a car containing the dials and gauges.

Dragster
A car made to compete in the sport of drag racing.

Exhaust
The fumes that leave the engine via the exhaust pipe.

Formula One
The highest level of motor racing, where drivers compete to be world champion.

Four-wheel drive
Where a car's engine drives all four wheels to give better grip.

Grille
Slats or mesh in front of the radiator, usually made of chrome.

Jet engine
An engine that pushes out fuel vapor and hot air. They are usually found on aircraft, but sometimes in cars.

Pollution
The damage caused to the environment by such things as vehicle exhaust.

Roll bar
An overhead bar that protects passengers if the car rolls over.

Solar panels
Panels that convert sunlight into electricity.

Spoiler
An aerodynamic device to push the car down on to the road

Speed of sound
The speed that sound travels through the air.

Stretch limousine
A luxury car made longer with the addition of a new center section.

Titanium
An expensive, light, and strong metal used in racing cars.

Whitewall tires
Tires with bands of white paint on the side. They were popular in the 1950s and 1960s.

Wind resistance
The force that opposes an object as it travels through the air.

Index